What Was It Like?™
PAUL REVERE

by Lawrence Weinberg
illustrated by Marie de John

CHILDRENS PRESS CHOICE
A Longmeadow title selected for educational distribution
ISBN 0-516-09557-9

Text copyright ©1988 Angel Entertainment, Inc.
Illustrations copyright ©1988 Marie de John. All rights reserved.
Cover artwork copyright ©1988 Julie Hodde.

Manufactured in the United States of America.

ello, I'm Paul Revere. Most of you have probably heard of my famous ride in 1776 from Boston to Lexington to warn the colonists that the Redcoats (the British) were coming. Although that is what I am most well-known for, I accomplished many other things. But I'm getting ahead of myself. Let me start at the beginning.

I grew up in Boston and went to school just like you do. We didn't get to stay home on Saturdays and during the summer, though. By the time we were seven or eight, our hard-working mothers and fathers wanted us where someone could keep an eye on us all day long. They had good reason, too. Left alone for a minute, my friends and I would go down to the waterfront and climb up the tall masts of the sailing ships (whenever the captains would let us, and sometimes even when they wouldn't!).

We also loved to fish. We would row out in the Boston Harbor whenever we got the chance to borrow a boat. Sometimes, when the weather was bad, the water got rough. You had to be a good swimmer in case the boat turned over.

We played in the narrow streets, too, near Clark's wharf where I lived. There was nothing dangerous about kicking a ball—unless you

weren't watching out for the wheels of the big horse carts. They carried barrels of molasses and sugar away from the ships that had just returned from the West Indies, as well as paper, glass, tea and coffee and all sorts of other things that had come from England.

We played safer games, too, like rolling marbles or flying kites off windy Beacon Hill. In the winter, we went ice skating on the pond in Boston Common. Our parents were glad to get us out of harm's way and into the classrooms.

There weren't many public schools then. My father, who was named Paul Revere, too, had to pay two cents a week to send me to a private school. It was a school for the sons of tradesmen, or artisans as they were called then. They were the men who ran the stores and shops, including bakers, printers, candlemakers and silversmiths.

Unlike us, boys from wealthy families went to what was called a Latin School. They learned all sorts of things I never had a chance to learn, such as the Greek and Latin languages. Then, if they were smart enough to become lawyers, doctors or ministers, they went on to college at Harvard. We tradesmen's sons were only expected to learn reading, writing and arithmetic. Then, when we turned twelve or thirteen, we were supposed to start getting a different kind of education—we became apprentices and learned how to earn a living by working all day in our fathers' shops!

That didn't mean that a person had to be ignorant for the rest of his life. Anyone could do what Ben Franklin had done when he left school in Boston—beg, borrow or buy books on every subject under the sun, from science to poetry, and start to learn on his own.

I loved books as much as Ben Franklin did. I spent most of my time in my father's shop, however. He was a silversmith, and he made all sorts of lovely things out of the gold and silver his customers brought to our little shop on Fish Street. You name it, and my father could make it. Sitting at his workbench, he could create just about anything from jewelry to punchbowls. He made fancy belt buckles, too, and the spurs men wore on their boots.

I wanted to learn everything that he knew. But before he started teaching me, I had to sign a contract. It stated that I would be his apprentice until I was twenty-one years old. During that time, I'd have to obey him in everything. And what's more, he didn't even have to pay me while I was working for him. All I was supposed to get for my work was the same room, food and clothing he had always given me.

He wasn't being hard on me. Other tradesmen's sons had the same situation with their fathers, or whomever else they were apprenticed to. My father himself had become an apprentice to a master silversmith when he was thirteen. Not only did that man pay him nothing during all those years, but it was my father who had to pay the man in order to be his apprentice. That sounds unfair, except that he learned from that man how to become a master silversmith. Now he was passing on to me all that he had been taught.

From sunup to sundown, we worked together in my father's small shop. It was crowded with three-legged stools, tubs of water, workbenches and metal-covered anvils for hammering the silver and gold. There were tools everywhere and at one side of the room was a furnace that melted the silver and gold we formed into all sorts of different objects.

When I started my apprenticeship, one of my main jobs was to pump the bellows to blow air into the fire. The air fanned the flames to make the fire hot enough to melt the silver or gold. My father worked on the melted ores in a container called a crucible. When it was hot, he could form it into any shape he wanted to before it cooled again.

I swept and ran errands, too, but mostly I watched my father very carefully. Then, little by little, he began to trust me enough to help him roll the precious silver into sheets, cut it into forms and hammer it with mallets.

Father was always very careful never to waste anything. I suppose that was why he gave me such a strange pair of leather pants to wear under my leather apron. They were so big and floppy that after I had worn down the side I was always sitting on, I could turn them around and then start sitting on the front side.

I was learning a lot, but there I was, fifteen-years-old, with no spending money to go out with my friends. I couldn't ask my father for money, since I had two younger brothers and four sisters he had to support, too. So I decided to find myself an extra job. I became a part-time bell ringer. If Boston had a lot of anything in those days, it was churches. All the churches had bells, but the most beautiful-sounding church bells you could ever hear, all eight of them, were in the tower of Christ Church. When

they rang out, people all over Boston stopped to listen. I was very excited when the master bell ringer hired seven of us to help him pull the long ropes that made the bells clang. We had to do a lot of practicing because pulling those ropes wasn't nearly as easy as it sounds. There's a trick to just about everything, you know, if you want to be good at it. Each of those bells sounded differently and had to be pulled at just the right time or the music would come out all wrong.

We were so proud of what we were doing that we called ourselves the "Bell Ringers Society." Ringing was very important in those days. Church bells didn't just call people to prayer services, even though there were a lot of those! They also rang out whenever something important was happening in town, from a fire to a celebration. I loved to ring the bells. And sometimes when all was quiet, I liked to climb the winding stairs up to the top of the bell tower. It was the highest place in Boston. From there I could look out over the whole city—even across the Charles River into the town of Cambridge.

When I was nineteen, my father died. As the eldest son, I had to be strong for my family. I couldn't take over my father's business, though, because I wasn't twenty-one years old yet, and had not served the required seven years as an apprentice. My mother could run the shop, though, for two years, and I would do all the actual work with my younger brother Thomas. Then, when I turned twenty-one, I could take over from my mother and run it myself.

The shop did a lot of business, even without my father. People kept bringing their silver and gold, despite my inexperience. They could see that I was used to working hard, and that my father had taught me well.

I enjoyed working in the shop and teaching my brother Thomas what my father had taught me. I had a lot of responsibility, though, and had to grow up fast. I had to stand by my mother and keep my brothers and sisters in line. I also felt a responsibility to protect Massachusetts. When I was twenty-one, I did what most young men in Boston did, and joined the army to fight the French. France ruled Canada and was trying to move down into what are now America's midwestern states. England, who owned the Colonies, considered this land hers. There were also a great many Colonial settlers in the western wilderness. France, with the help of Indians, attacked our settlers.

I must admit that I also wanted a little adven-

ture. I wanted to see more of the world. If I didn't go now, I would be married with a family of my own, without having ever left the town of Boston.

At first, I couldn't have been happier that I was going off to war. The men were allowed to help pick their own officers, and I was made a second lieutenant! When we marched west, folks in the towns came out to wish us well. We marched past fields and woods, over the Berkshire Mountains, and crossed the Hudson River into Albany, New York. There, we met with militiamen who had come up from other Colonies to join us.

At first, we weren't sure how much we liked each other. We were used to thinking of people from New York and Connecticut and the other Colonies as if they were from other countries. We all wanted the same thing, though—to start defending the settlers. But, we had to wait in Albany because the British General who was to command us wasn't there. Our orders were to do nothing until he arrived with his own troops.

When the English officers finally appeared, they took one look at us and turned up their noses. They thought we were nothing but riff-raff because we all wore homespun clothes

instead of beautiful red uniforms like their own men, and because we couldn't march in step. It is true that their officers knew more about soldiering, since that was what they did for a living. We were only young men from shops and farms.

Finally, we got the orders to form ranks and move out. Our spirits rose as we marched north to the shores of Lake George. But, as soon as we got there, we were all commanded to move into Fort William Henry, at the head of Lake George, and stay there.

Meanwhile, the enemy was *still* attacking the settlers. Flies and mosquitoes swarmed into our camp by the millions. The camp was very dirty. Sickness and diseases began to spread, and soldiers started to die right and left without ever even having the chance to fight. We buried at least five men a day.

Then the French and their Indian allies came. They raided us in small parties, picking us off one by one with muskets and bows and arrows.

It was almost winter, and we didn't have any warm clothes. Luckily, the French were in no mood to fight in the snow and icy winds. When they pulled back to their camps in Canada, the British General told us that we wouldn't be needed again until Spring. We carried our wounded and set off in rags for home.

On the long walk back, I began to wonder if I really wanted to call myself an Englishman. We had been treated very badly by the officers of the British Army.

I started to think that those militiamen from the other Colonies were a lot more like our boys from Massachusetts. They were simple folk, as we were, who had left their farms and shops to risk their lives.

I went back to the workbench in my shop. I fell in love with Sara Orne. I would take her rowing in Boston Harbor. Soon we were married. Over the years, we had eight children (only six survived past infancy) and lived peacefully.

Peace did not last long in Boston, though. The war with France had cost England a lot of money. The English felt that since they had protected us from the French we should help them pay for the war. They didn't ask *our* opinion, though.

Unlike many of the Colonies, Massachusetts had traded with many other countries besides England. Boston sailing ships had been able to roam the oceans and trade wherever they pleased. Now, however, England wanted to control the trade in and out of Boston. The new King of England, George the Third, began to enforce an old law called the Navigation Act.

The major idea behind the Act was to keep Boston from buying anything that didn't come *from* England and to keep them from selling anything to any other country *but* England. The King hired a native Bostonian, Charles Paxton, as Customs Official to make sure we obeyed the Navigation Act. Paxton wanted to take any people who disregarded the Act to court. But, when he did, no Boston jury would convict them. Paxton established Admirality Courts. They had no juries, just a judge, but Paxton still needed evidence. His men boarded our ships to look for smuggled goods, and even broke into our homes. When we questioned their right to search our homes, they waved pieces of paper called Writs of Assistance which stated that the law permitted them to go right ahead.

I felt that these laws were unfair, though I didn't know what I could do about them. A man named Sam Adams believed that we could, and should, do something to show the King we wouldn't stand for his unfair taxes. Sam and I were both members of the Freemasons. The Masons, as we were called, believed in a democratic society in which all men were free. Masons promoted the idea of the brotherhood of man. I had joined the year before, in 1760, and met the great thinkers of Boston, like Sam Adams, his cousin John, John Warren and John Hancock. I was a man of action, by nature. I loved to get things done. The Masons shared my ideas about freedom, and they needed someone like me who could take charge and put those thoughts into action. As an artisan, I also knew a lot of other artisans who would be interested in doing something for the cause of liberty. I was a valuable friend to Sam and John Adams.

In the meantime, King George had the English Parliament pass a law putting a high tax on every barrel of molasses that was imported into the Colonies. Molasses happened to be the main commodity that our ships brought here. It was used to make rum, and the rum was then shipped across the ocean and sold to pay for other goods the Colonies needed.

Then, in 1763, Boston was struck with the deadly disease, smallpox. It is no longer the threat it used to be because you get vaccinated for it when you are very young. The vaccination for smallpox had been introduced in Boston during the last outbreak forty years earlier, but

17

many people were too scared to try it. As a result, they came down with the disease.

In 1763, one of my children was among the first smallpox victims in Boston. In those days, people with smallpox had two choices. They could go to a hospital, called a pesthouse. The chances for recovery in a pesthouse were very slim. Or, they could hang a flag outside their doors which told everybody that someone inside had the disease. A guard would then be posted to make sure that no one would go in or out of the house. I would not let my child go to almost certain death in a pesthouse, and so I hung a flag on my doorway.

Soon, all these precautions didn't matter because half of Boston came down with smallpox. A few months later, people were desperate enough to try vaccination. This time it really worked! Soon the disease was gone and we could stop worrying about dying and begin worrying again about living under England's unfair rule.

A new tax law was passed in England in 1765, the Stamp Act. This law said that you had to buy a stamp if you wanted to buy a newspaper or write a legal or business document, such as a will or a bill of sale. The stamp, itself, was not something we needed in order to read a newspaer. But the King knew that everyone bought newspapers and wrote wills, so it was an easy way for him to make money.

I decided it was time for action.

I joined a brand new society that would *do* something. We called ourselves the Sons of Liberty. One night, some of our members went to a street corner in Boston and hung a dummy from a big elm tree. It looked just like the King's officer, Andrew Oliver, who was supposed to collect the stamp tax. We made another dummy of the English Lord who had first proposed the stamp tax. We put the devil's horns on his head, and stuck him in a giant boot.

The elm tree became known as the Liberty Tree. There was no other tree in history that caused so much trouble. Soon Liberty Trees were springing up in towns all over the Colonies.

At dusk that night, I joined a funeral procession, formed under the Liberty Tree, to burn the dummies. Afterwards, we marched to see the Royal Governor. We chanted outside his windows, "Liberty, property and no stamps! If we can't vote on taxes, then you can't tax us! Taxation without representation is tyranny!" Soon, people were repeating these words all over the Colonies. Just to make sure the King got the

message, Americans by the thousands found a way of voting against this hateful tax. They voted with their money, and vowed not to buy any British goods until the Stamp Tax was revoked.

Under pressure from English businessmen, the King repealed the Stamp Act before it went into effect. But he didn't give up trying to make money from the Colonies. The King and Parliament enacted some even harsher tax laws, the Townshend Acts. These Acts allowed the King to tax us when we bought tea, glass, paint and paper. He also sent two regiments of soldiers to Boston to keep an eye on the Sons of Liberty.

General Gage was the Commander in Chief of the British Army in the American Colonies. Gage moved to Boston from New York when his soldiers arrived from England. We liked the General well enough. He tried to keep the soldiers well-behaved. Gage didn't believe we were simple country bumpkins, as most of the other English officers did. He respected us, both as a people and as soldiers. He knew from having served in the French and Indian War, that we were better shots than his Redcoats.

We had no army barracks in Boston, so the soldiers lived wherever they could find room—

in warehouses, in tents on other people's lawns and even in the colonists' houses. Many colonists who were still loyal to England welcomed the soldiers in hopes that they would put a stop to the "rabble rousers." I suppose I was one of those rabble rousers because I didn't believe that England always knew what was best for us. I also firmly believed that we should be asked about issues that affected us. We didn't want the British soldiers taking charge in our town.

The people of Boston, however, did nothing violent to show that they were upset. We decided instead to make things as unpleasant as possible for the soldiers, hoping to make them give up and go away. Many British soldiers felt the way we did, and deserted. I actually helped many British soldiers change out of their red uniforms into Colonial farmers' clothes, so they could escape.

The British soldiers and the colonists lived in a state of uneasy peace for one-and-a-half years. With so much resentment on both sides, it was a wonder that no one got hurt sooner. The tension grew and grew until one cold day in March of 1770, a mob surrounded a British soldier on guard duty. People in the mob began to hurl snowballs and insults at him. Some children called him "Lobsterback" (because of his red uniform). The frustrated guard hit a boy. When the large angry crowd closed in on him, eight more soldiers rushed to the British guard's side. Someone in the crowd hit one of them with a stick of wood. Suddenly, it was a free-for-all. Everyone was struggling with everyone else. Out of the din, the command was heard, "Present arms." Then, the fatal command, "Fire!" No one knows who issued the order. The crowd retreated, but not before four people lay dead, and eight wounded, one of whom died.

This incident happened not far from my shop. I heard the ringing of bells and shouting. Thinking at first that a fire had broken out, I threw down my tools and grabbed a water bucket. Once I was out the door, I realized that the racket was not about a fire. People were shouting, "To arms! To arms! Fight the Redcoats!"

Everyone was furious. Back in my shop, I engraved a picture in copper of the Boston Massacre. Then I dipped the copper in ink and printed the pictures on paper.

My pictures of the killings were sold all over Boston. Horseback riders carried them to towns and villages throughout the Colonies. They even crossed the Atlantic to England, where many people were on our side in this tug-of-war with King George.

The soldiers were ordered to leave Boston and to move to Castle Island in Boston Harbor. King George eventually revoked the hated Townshend taxes. But, he didn't revoke everything. He left one tax—on tea. The amount of the tax was so small that he thought we wouldn't notice it. The King was lying low now until all the fuss died down in the Colonies. But this one tax was his way of saying that he still had the right to do with us as he chose. This tax on tea was a symbol of British authority.

We stopped boycotting and started importing British goods once more, however. People desperately needed to get back to work. Again, for a few years an uneasy peace settled in Boston. Merchants were trading again, the soldiers were gone and life continued. But, we didn't forget that tax on tea.

On September 15, 1772, my wife Sara had our eighth child. She was very weak after giving birth, and not strong enough to survive through the spring. The baby died shortly afterwards. I was left with six children to look after. One summer night, later that year, I was hurrying to get home before my children went to sleep when I bumped into a young woman named Rachel Walker. We liked each other immediately. A few months later, she agreed to become my wife.

In the meantime, the uneasy peace we had established with England was threatened once again. The great East India Company had forty million pounds of tea to sell, but nowhere to sell it. The British government gave them a monopoly in the American Colonies. This meant that only the East India Company could sell to the American Colonies, and no one else. The idea of a monopoly scared most people, including me. If England could give one company a monopoly on tea, would they do the same for other goods like shoes and cloth? Colonial merchants would not be able to do business if that happened.

Not long afterwards, three ships sailed into Boston Harbor loaded down with East India Company tea. We were determined to make the ships return to England with their tea still aboard. Under Massachusetts law, it was illegal for a ship to leave the harbor without unloading. They also had to leave within twenty days or the goods could be taken by the government. The Governor wouldn't allow the ships to leave. After eighteen days of trying to convince the Governor to let the ships leave unloaded, the

Sons of Liberty were ready to do something more drastic.

We decided to hold a tea party, and use Boston Harbor as the teapot! That December night one hundred and fifty of us went down to Griffin Wharf. We covered our faces with charcoal soot and candle-grease war paint. We stuck chicken feathers out of our stocking caps. We wrapped blankets around ourselves and held hatchets in our hands. Maybe we didn't look like real Indians, but we were certainly frightening.

We separated into three groups at the wharf, one for each ship. I led one group. I rushed up to the first mate of the ship and held out my hand. He handed me the keys to the storeroom where the tea was kept. My men lost no time in carrying the heavy chests up to the deck. We pried them open and heaved the tea into the salt water of the harbor.

We had to work fast, as well as silently. British warships were anchored in the water not far away. Meanwhile, hundreds of townspeople had followed us to Griffin Wharf. Soon, there were thousands more. For hours, they stood quietly along the shore, watching us.

It was almost dawn before we finished, and returned wearily to our homes. I never got to

sleep, though. My horse was waiting for me, saddled and ready. There were other Sons of Liberty in New York City and Philadelphia who had to be told about the "Boston Tea Party," as we called our tea dumping that night. The night was cold, the roads icy. I had three hundred and fifty long miles to ride each way on my journey.

When I returned to Boston, people began calling me "Bold Revere" for my part in the Boston Tea Party, as well as my fast riding. I brought good news back to Boston. The Sons of Liberty in both New York and Philadelphia were willing to stand behind us. They thought we had done the right thing by throwing that East India tea overboard.

If our boycott of English goods had angered King George, the Boston Tea Party had made him ready to explode. General Gage was ordered to replace the Royal Governor and take over Boston. The King also ordered that until the tea that had been thrown overboard was paid for, not one ship, ferry or rowboat was allowed to go in or out of Boston Harbor. That was bad news for us. Almost all our food and goods came by water, and everything we sold went by water. We were in terrible trouble. Soon it could get worse if the General sent his soldiers to block the one road that led out of Boston. Then we would all starve—unless we surrendered.

I left Boston to tell the Colonies what the British were doing. Most colonists were behind us because they knew that if Boston were starved into surrendering, they could be next. Everywhere I went, people were ready to help us so that we did not starve. Other New England Colonies sent us codfish and corn. Charlestown, South Carolina sent rice, Baltimore, Maryland, sent bread and Philadelphia, Pennsylvania sent money.

General Gage brought in eleven regiments of soldiers to keep order in Boston. Town meetings had already been prohibited by England. But, colonists had regarded these meetings as a God-given right. We would not let England get away with this. We called a county meeting in Suffolk County. We decided that if the situation continued, we might have to revolt. You can be sure that Sam Adams had a lot to say at this meeting.

Next, I rode to Philadelphia, where the First Continental Congress was meeting. Leaders from all the Colonies had come to discuss the growing problems with England. I brought copies of our decisions at the Suffolk County meeting.

Not everyone in the Congress agreed with our

revolutionary statements. Congress voted, however, to come to Boston's defense—if the British started the fighting, that is.

I, along with three other men, spent the winter watching every move of the British soldiers. As spies, we patroled the streets all night. We always knew where the British were.

Meanwhile, the British government was upset over General Gage's lack of action. As spring drew near, Gage knew it was time to act. He was determined to finally capture some of the rebel leaders. He decided on Sam Adams and John Hancock. They were both hiding in Lexington. Gage also knew that gunpowder and guns had been hidden in the Massachusetts' towns of Worcester and Concord. He decided to raid Concord. By the fifteenth of April, 1775, my friends and I knew that the general was planning something big. Three days later, on the eighteenth, we were aware that he was going to send out his troops that night. I didn't know whether the soldiers would leave Boston by sea, sailing boats across the Charles River, or by land, marching along the Neck Road. I learned now that they were to go by sea.

I sent one of our riders, Billy Dawes, to ride out through the British sentries along the Neck and relay the warning to Lexington and Concord. If anyone could make it past the sentries, it was Dawes. He was a born actor. I was going to row across the Charles River, past the British ships anchored there. I knew that both of us were in great danger. By now, I was well-known to General Gage as a messenger. He knew I would try to spread the news of the invasion. His men would be watching for me. I had to make sure that even if Billy Dawes and I were caught, the warnings would still be sent to Lexington and Concord. I arranged for another signal to be sent.

Robert Newton, the sexton of Christ Church, was to go up to the top of the bell tower with two lanterns. He was to light one if the enemy was going by land, two if by water. Now that I knew they were going by water, I had to tell Newton so he could light the two lanterns.

When I reached his house, it was full of British officers who were living there. I couldn't just walk up and knock on his door. I didn't know what I was going to do. Suddenly, Newton stepped out of a hiding place in the shadows of the street.

Quickly, I told him to climb up the bell tower and light two lanterns. Two other men and I

hurried to the wharf where my rowboat was hidden. In my haste, I forgot my spurs and some cloth with which to muffle the oars of the rowboat. It was lucky that my dog had followed me to the wharf. I tied a note around his collar and sent him home to Rachel. The dog was back in no time with my spurs.

There was a girl we knew who lived near the wharf. We went to her window and whistled. When she heard what we wanted, she ducked back inside the house for a moment, took off the flannel petticoat she'd been wearing beneath her skirt and threw it to us. We used it to muffle the oars and managed to row right past the guns of the British ship Somerset, which was there to make sure that men like me stayed in Boston.

We arrived safely in Charleston on the other side of the river. I rode on alone. I had to gallop across open fields, where I could be seen in the moonlight. But, if I stayed in the shadows, I could ride right into an ambush.

Suddenly, I saw something gleaming and I brought my horse to a stop. I realized it was a pistol holster. As I made my dash, two officers galloped out of an ambush. One came straight at me. The other went further down the road to cut me off in case I got past the first one.

But I didn't go further down the road. I galloped off cross-country and onto another road. The village of Medford was ahead of me, its houses dark. Riding full speed until I came to the home of the captain of the Medford minutemen, I leaned from my saddle to hammer on the door.

"The Regulars are coming this way!" I shouted. "They're heading for Concord! Muster your men!"

I galloped onward towards Lexington and Concord. I spread the alarm wherever I went. Reaching Lexington by midnight, I leaped off my horse in front of the house where John Adams and John Hancock were sleeping. I warned them to leave as quickly as possible.

While the two men were getting ready, William Dawes arrived safely. He'd narrowly escaped, too. Together, we set out for Concord. A young doctor named Samuel Prescott joined us. Halfway to the town, Prescott and Dawes stopped at another house to spread the alarm. I was about two-hundred yards in front of them when some British soldiers surrounded me. They weren't looking for Prescott, and in the darkness he managed to slip away. He rode on to alarm the minutemen at Concord to prepare to

fight. Dawes never made it to Concord.

Meanwhile, I was a prisoner. I didn't know whether I was going to be shot then and there, or taken back to Boston to be hanged. We heard a gun being fired. I told the soldiers that all over the countryside people had been warned of the British arrival. The soldiers knew they had to get back because there would be fighting soon. They took my horse and galloped off to find the rest of the British troops, leaving me behind.

I made my way back to Lexington. There, I learned from John Lowell, John Hancock's clerk, that a trunk full of important papers had been left in Lexington. If the British found the trunk, they could locate some of our men in Boston. It was at Buckman's Tavern, where Lowell had stayed. As we carried it out of the house, the British arrived. We crossed between the Redcoats and a much smaller line of our own minutemen to get away with the trunk. Suddenly, behind us, I heard a gun fire. The Redcoats and minutemen had opened fire on one another.

That was the first shot of the American Revolution—"a shot heard 'round the world." The British soldiers swept past our fallen lads and hurried on to Concord, but the colonists had already been alarmed and managed to remove

the guns and ammunition. Finding no colonists to fight, the British began marching back to Boston.

But they were in for a big surprise. Hundreds of minutemen lurked behind trees and inside farmhouses. The minutemen shot at the British soldiers who were marching down the middle of the road. It was very easy for the minutemen to pick off many British because the Redcoats had nowhere to run. The minutemen, meanwhile, were out of sight, so the British had nothing to aim at. This was the beginning of a war that would not end until we had freed our land from British rule.

At the Second Continental Congress, soon after the Battles of Lexington and Concord, as they came to be called, George Washington was elected Commander in Chief of the Continental Army. Most of the rebels, including myself, had to move out of Boston because the British now controlled the city. I had to leave all of my silver-smithing tools behind. I took odd jobs to make money to feed my family and support the Revolution. I printed paper money in Massachusetts and delivered messages all over New England and Pennsylvania.

Then, in November, General George

Washington assigned me a new job. The Battle of Bunker Hill was our first big loss. But the Revolutionary Army had withstood three attacks by a larger number of British soldiers before falling. It was not our lack of courage or fighting skills that lost that battle. We lost the Battle of Bunker Hill because we had run out of gunpowder. Our army desperately needed powder. There were very few gunpowder factories in the Colonies (the best were in Philadelphia), but none of them could make enough to supply the army. I rode to Philadelphia to tour a powder mill and to learn how to make gunpowder. I planned to open a plant in Massachusetts. The owner of the mill, Captain Eve, was not very patriotic. He was more concerned with profit and didn't want someone else, namely me, to set up a mill to compete with his. He couldn't refuse to let me tour his mill, but he wouldn't let me ask any questions or talk to any of the workmen.

I walked as slowly as I could, and tried to memorize everything I saw. Then, I went back to Massachusetts, and proceeded to build a gunpowder plant in the town of Canton, a few miles outside of Boston.

In April 1776, the British evacuated Boston, and we moved back into the city. I was commissioned as a major in the militia that was to defend Boston. Then I was promoted to lieutenant colonel and commander at Castle Island in Boston Harbor, where I served for three years.

On July 4, 1776, the Declaration of Independence was signed. This famous document, written by Thomas Jefferson, did not have any direct effect on the outcome of the battles, although it did do a lot for the morale of the Revolutionary Army. We were fighting for a goal now—independence and freedom. The Declaration of Independence also let England know that we were not backing down.

In 1777, the army called on me for a different reason. We needed cannons. So I started to build them. Then, one day, a British warship was wrecked in a storm off Cape Cod. It was the Somerset, the same ship that I'd had to row so quietly past the night before I started my ride to Lexington. We hauled all of its cannons onto shore, and then set them up in Boston Harbor to protect the town.

The Battle of Saratoga was the turning point of the Revolution. Two British Generals tried to divide the Colonies, in order to conquer them more easily. One General failed. On October 17, 1777, the British General surrendered to General Horatio Gates at Saratoga. This was a very important victory for the colonists because it allowed Benjamin Franklin to convince the French that there was a chance that we could win this war with England. In 1778, France entered into an alliance with the Colonies. Without French help we might not have won the war.

On October 17-19, 1781, the British General Cornwallis surrendered to General George Washington at Yorktown. The fighting was over. A little more than eight years after that first shot on the Lexington Green, peace was finally declared between England and the United States of America! The Treaty of Paris in 1783 formally recognized the new nation.

Everyone celebrated. I returned to silversmithing with my sons, Paul and John Warren, who were now my apprentices. We made many more teapots and silver bowls. I also began making eyeglasses, anvils, hammers, stoves and silver bells. My first bell was for the Second Church in Boston. Over the years, John Warren and I made hundreds of bells for steeples throughout the Colonies.

I lived a full and rewarding life. I loved silversmithing, and no matter how many other things I tried—delivering messages, making gunpowder and cannons. I always returned to silversmithing, and I passed my skills on to my children. The most important part of my life, however, was my contribution to the birth of this great nation. The ride for a free America I began on the night of April 18, 1775, has not yet ended. It has really just begun. Now it is your turn to make your own ride to help all Americans everywhere to remain free.

The Life and Times
of Paul Revere

1735 On January 1, Paul Revere is born in Boston, in the British Colony of Massachusetts.

1754 On July 22, Paul's father dies.

1756 In the spring, Paul becomes a second lieutenant in the Massachusetts militia during the French and Indian War.

1757 Paul marries Sara Orne in August.

1764 Smallpox breaks out in Boston.

1765 August 13-14, the Sons of Liberty hang in effigy the collector of the Stamp Act tax, and march in protest on the Town House, the seat of the Massachusetts Colonial government.

1768 On September 30, British troops occupy Boston, where everyone is seething over the Townshend Acts.

1770 On March 5, British soldiers fire at an angry crowd in Boston. On that same day, in England, Parliament votes to repeal the Townshend Acts.

1773 Sara Orne dies on May 3.
Paul marries Rachel Walker on September 23. On December 16-17, Paul helps to lead the Boston Tea Party. They board

three ships at Griffin's Wharf and dump 342 chests of tea overboard.

1774   In the fall, a county meeting is held in Suffolk County, Massachusetts. It adopts the Suffolk Resolves, which Paul carries to the First Continental Congress, in Philadelphia, Pennsylvania. Congress adopts this promise to come to the aid of Boston if attacked by British troops.

1775   On April 18-19, Paul rides during the night to Lexington, Massachusetts, to warn of the approach of British troops from Boston.

1776   In April, Lieutenant Colonel Paul Revere is stationed at Castle William, a former British fort, to guard Boston Harbor. He later assumes command there.

1779   After serving on an unsuccessful expedition to Maine, Paul is court-martialed for disobedience, and found innocent.

1783   On September 3, peace is formally declared between England and the United States of America. The Revolutionary War is over.

1792   Paul casts his first bell.

1818   On May 10, Paul dies.